Inspirational & Wisdom Sayings of African American Men

Helen L. Bevel

Birth Of A Civilization Series
Inspirational & Wisdom Sayings of African American Men

ISBN: 978-1-105-15423-2

Published by
The Institute for the Study and Advancement of Nonviolence
http://almanac.2freedom.com nonviolentstudy@gmail.com • (773) 413-0081
(202) 527-9798 • Fax (267) 695-8267

DEDICATED TO

"To those who are just entering life; upon whom the freshness and joy of youth still rest, I would say, life is fleeting and it is hardly worth while to follow anything but that which makes for the up building of humanity. Fill your life with love and righteousness, with meekness and peacemaking, with humbleness of heart, with faithful work for God and man."

—Edward Wilmot Blyden, 1832-1912

INTRODUCTION

The following pages are filled with quotes, sayings, and prescriptions for living life. The African American men featured have overcome great odds and challenges to bring these word gems to us. It is my prayer that all African American males young and old will be enriched by this compilation from some of the greatest that have set foot on the shores of the Americas.

To the fatherless boy or man, know that within you lies the seed of your ancestors, maybe one of these yet unknown. As many were able to overcome the horrors and atrocities of slavery and achieve greatness so can you. It is all there in your heart. Circumstances and conditions you can overcome as many of these featured brothers have proven.

Though they may have erred and fallen short in many ways, they overcame the mandate of destruction, and for this we are grateful. Behavior is but a conditioning and we must remember the road they trod and the conditions they were confronted with.

There are many races and nations of people who are now extinct as a result of having encountered the European, but these our brothers, fathers, husbands and sons have overcome and achieved a semblance of purpose, a fulfilling of a higher design orchestrated by the Creator.

May these inspirational quotes and sayings edify your soul, uplift your spirit, penetrate your mind, purge your emotions and activate your body to move towards the "High Calling" that is yours. To fulfill your destiny and purpose for Being.

Throw off the shackles of fear. Loosen the chains of doubt. Eradicate the noose of inferiority, step out of the jail of anger and be the Light that shines in the darkness. Let your sunlight shine, for you are moon to no man. You are the "Light of the World."

We your mothers, sisters, wives, daughters and kin need you to help return us to a civilized way of living, a life of peace, prospertity and justice. A way akin to that of our ancient ancestors who brought math, science, astronomy, pyramids, culture, agriculture and language to the world. You are here for a "Divine Purpose." It is your time. Rise!

Infinite Love and Gratitude,

Myeka

"The choice is not between non-violence and violence, but between non-violence and non-existence."

"Now, I say to you today my friends, even though we face the difficulties of today and tomorrow, I still have a dream. It is a dream deeply rooted in the American dream. I have a dream that one day this nation will rise up and live out the true meaning of its creed: We hold these truths to be self-evident, that all men are created equal."

"If the Negro is to be free he must move down into the inner resources of his own soul and sign with the pen and ink of self asserted manhood, his own Emancipation Proclamation."

"Hate destroys a man's sense of values and his objectivity. It causes him to describe the beautiful as ugly and the ugly as beautiful, and to confuse the true with the false and the false with the true."

"We have flown the air like birds and swum the sea like fish, but we have yet to learn the simple act of walking the earth like brothers."

The Negro needs the white man to free him from his fears. The white man needs the Negro to free him from his guilt."

"Cowardice asks the question - is it safe?
Expediency asks the question - is it polite?
Vanity asks the question - is it popular?
But conscience asks the question - is it right?
And there comes a time when one must take a position that is neither safe, nor polite, nor popular but one must take it because it is right."

"A nation that spends more on military than on social programs and education is morally bankrupt."

—Dr. Martin Luther King, Jr

"The best way to not feel hopeless is to get up and do something. Don't wait for good things to happen to you. If you go out and make some good things happen, you will fill the world with hope, you will fill yourself with hope."

"Change will not come if we wait for some other time. We are the ones we've been waiting for. We are the change that we seek."

—President Barack H. Obama

Nguzo Saba Seven Principles of Kwanzaa

1.UMOJA (Unity)
2.KUJICHAGULIA (self-determination)
3.UJIMA (Collective Work & Responsibility)
4.UJAMAA (Cooperative Economics)
5.NIA (Purpose)
6.KUUMBA (Creativity)
7.IMANI (Faith)

"It is Martin King who taught that a real moral struggle seeks to win partners, not to leave victims."

—Dr. Maulana "Ron" Karenga

"In life we don't get what we want, we get in life what we are. If we want more we have to be able to be more, in order to be more you have to face rejection."

—Farah Gray, Self-made millionaire at age 14, 1984-Present

"Success is measured by the impact I make everyday."

"Entrepreneurship can begin at any age. I committed to my dream at the age of nine, and was a millionaire by age 16."

—Ephren W. Taylor II, 1982-Present

"All that glamour builds up a false sense of ego. It's not needed. I'm already happy with who I am. My job is just to get on the podium."

—Shani Davis, Olympic Speed Skating Gold Medalist, 1982-Present

"Everything negative—pressure, challenges—is all an opportunity for me to rise."

—Kobe Bryant, 1978-Present

"One of the things that my parents have taught me is never listen to other people's expectations. You should live your own life and live up to your own expectations, and those are the only things I really care about it."

"Don't force your kids into sports. I never was. It's the child's desire to play that matters, not the parent's desire to have the child play. Fun. Keep it fun."

—Tiger Woods, 1975-Present

"Excellence is not a singular act but a habit. You are what you do repeatedly."

—Shaquille O'Neal, 1972-Present

Believe in something Believe in yourself Turn adversity into ambition. Now blossom into wealth.

—Tupac Shakur, 1971-Present

"I will not lose, for even in defeat, there's a valuable lesson learned, so it evens up for me."

"Remind yourself. Nobody built like you, you design yourself."

—JZ, 1969 - Present

"If you enter the world knowing you are loved and you leave the world knowing the same, then everything that happens in between can be dealt with."

"Children show me in their playful smiles the divine in everyone. This simple goodness shines straight from their hearts and only asks to be lived."

"There's a Mother's Day and there's a Father's Day, but there's no Children's Day. It would mean a lot. World peace."

"Let us dream of tomorrow where we can truly love from the soul, and know love as the ultimate truth at the heart of all creation."

—Michael Jackson, 1958-2009

"Successful people do more than talk, we act on our ideas and find out how to execute them."

—Omar Tyree, 1969-Present

"Throughout life people will make you mad, disrespect you and treat you bad. Let God deal with the things they do, cause hate in your heart will consume you."

"Greatness lives on the edge of destruction."

—Will Smith, 1968-Present

"Pursue your passion all the way. The thing you are most passionate about will bring the greatest rewards in life."

—Maurice Ashley, Int'l Grandmaster of Chess, 1966-Present

"Nonviolence is a way of life that will guarantee peaceful coexistence in the future and the eventual goal of a demilitarized region."

Congressman Jessie Jackson, Jr., 1965– Present

"I have always been motivated by a strong keen desire for true independence and a sense of achievement."

"If you have a core set of values like family, hard work, trust, these will stay with you even when you have difficulties.

—Reginald Lewis, TLC Beatrice Int'l Food, 1965-1993

"My attitude is that if you push me towards something that you think is a weakness, then I will turn that perceived weakness into a strength."

—Michael Jordan, 1963-Present

"Black people were stripped of an identity when brought here, and it's been a quest since then to define who we are."

"Our greatness, our talent has never been the question. It's been a matter of grappling for control over what we do."

"It is really important that young people find something that they want to do and pursue it with passion. I'm very passionate about filmmaking. It's what I love to do."

—Spike Lee, 1957-Present

"Judgment of the people in the situation is not helpful. How can you help them is the question."

"The key ingredient to any kind of happiness or success is to never give less than your best."

—Russell Simmons, 1957—Present

"Most important, if you love someone, tell him or her, for you never know what tomorrow may have in store."

—Walter Payton, 1954 - 1999

"I made a commitment to completely cut out drinking and anything that might hamper me from getting my mind and body together. And the floodgates of goodness have opened upon me - spiritually and financially."

—Denzel Washington, 1954 - Present

"Elie Wiesel says that the greatest evil in the world is not anger or hatred, but indifference. If that is true, then the opposite is also true: that the greatest love we can show our children is the attention we pay them, the time we take for them. Maybe we serve children the best simply by noticing them."

"Do you see law and order? There is nothing but disorder, and instead of law there is the illusion of security. It is an illusion because it is built on a long history of injustices: racism, criminality, and the genocide of millions. Many people say it is insane to resist the system, but actually, it is insane not to."

"I spend my days preparing for life, not preparing for death… I believe in life, I believe in freedom, so my mind is not consumed with death. It's with love, life and those things. In many ways, on many days, only my body is here, because I am thinking about what's happening around the world."

—Mumia Abu-Jamal, 1954 - Present

"You can't lead the people if you don't love the people. You can't save the people if you don't serve the people."

—Dr. Cornell West, 1953 - Present

"In the pursuit of opportunity and success, we all need a greater adherence to principles and values in guiding our behavior and actions. I owe a great part of my success in business to a simple, personal philosophy: I believe you can be the most determined competitor, totally focused on winning, which I am, but you can do it with integrity, grace, and always treating people with respect and dignity."

—*Kenneth Irvine Chenault, 1951 - Present*

"What is important what I consider success is that we make a contribution to our world."

"To THINK BIG and to use our talents doesn't mean we won't have difficulties along the way. We will--we all do. If we choose to see the obstacles in our path as barriers, we stop trying. "We can't win," we moan. "They won't let us win."

—*Dr. Ben Carson, 1951 - Present*

"A leaders private and public life should be similar."

—*Swami Krishnapada, 1951 - 2005*

"Humanity is but a brief flicker in the history of the earth. The scale of the universe is unimaginably vast in as compared to what we are on the earth."

"Are we capable of being technological and not destroy ourselves?"

—*Gibor Basri, 1951 – Present*

"Ability may get you to the top, but it takes character to keep you there."

—*Stevie Wonder, 1950 - Present*

"No one can do everything, but everyone can do something."

—*Gil Scott-Heron, 1949 - Present*

I think segregation is bad, I think it's wrong, it's immoral. I'd fight against it with every breath in my body, but you don't need to sit next to a white person to learn how to read and write."

"Good manners will open doors that the best education cannot."

"I don't believe in quotas. America was founded on a philosophy of individual rights, not group rights."

—*Supreme Court Justice Clarence Thomas, 1948 - Present*

"I don't think you can compromise ... news either has integrity or it doesn't, ... It either is accurate, balanced and fair or it isn't."

–Richard Parsons

"You can't have civilization between a group of people who are not civil."

"Our greatest natural resource is not oil, wind power or trees, but rather the single greatest natural resource in the world is our youth."

—Bhagwan Ra Africa, 1948 - Present

"I can do something besides stuff a ball through a hoop. My greatest resource is my mind."

—Kareem Abdul-Jabbar, 1947 - Present

"The wise man listens while he speaks so he learns as her speaks."

"You can tell you what to do, but will you make you obey you in the things that are good for you."

-Yusuf Ali El, 1947 - Present

"If we talk about literacy, we have to talk about how to enhance our children's mastery over the tools needed to live intelligent, creative, and involved lives."

—Danny Glover

"One should begin by examining within self in order to find true corrective action to a problem that is threatening the mental, physical and spiritual existence of Man, He and She."

—High Priest Kwatamani, 1946 - Present

"Growing up Black and poor in America is clearly a challenge. But it's a challenge, which can be overcome as many have already done."

—Robert L. Johnson, 1946 - Present

"I feel that the most important requirement in success is learning to overcome failure. You must learn to tolerate it, but never accept it."

—Reggie Jackson, 1946 - Present

"As long as the colored man looks to white folks to put the crown on what he says, as long as he looks to white folks for approval, then he won't find out who he is and what he's about."

—August Wilson, Jr., 1945 - 2005

"The vast majority of white people are racist because of their own insecurity, they don't trust their own capabilities, despite the fact that the whole culture tells them how powerful they are. So when you begin to give those people ideas and indications of black genius it will frighten them and they will become even more strident, even more vehement, even more determined in their determination to be racist. That's a large number of them. Then there is another group of racists who are sick, who are so sick that it doesn't matter what you tell them, what they see, what they understand, they're gonna maintain beyond a shadow of a doubt, the total inferiority of everybody black, and the total superiority of everybody white. Now that's a very sick racist. That's the kind of racist who will see genius and call it ignorance. That's the kind of racist that will see power and call it weakness. That's the kind of racist that will see intelligence and call it unintelligence. That's the kind of racist that will get very clear information and will be unable to change their own conduct.................."

"When our young people know that there are no limits to their potential in the world of manufacturing, communication, physics, chemistry or the science of the human mind, then those same young Black minds ... will recreate these fields of human endeavor with the same incomparability as on the basketball courts we create the athletic genius of Michael Jordan or Magic Johnson... "

"Human beings are unable to be about the serious business of living and building societies if they feel compelled to always clown or entertain others. People do not take you seriously if you don't take yourself seriously. A sense of humor brings necessary balance to an organized life, but a life of humor blinds one to life."

"You must structure your world so that you are constantly reminded of who you are."

—Dr. Na'im Akbar, 1944 - Present

"Africa Unite."

"Don't gain the world and lose your soul, wisdom is better than silver or gold."

"The greatness of a man is not in how much wealth is acquired, but in his integrity and his ability to affect those around him positively."

—Bob Marley, 1945 - 1981

"Now consciousness, what is consciousness? Consciousness is being aware of one's surroundings, recognizing the existence, truth or fact of something; being aware of the very moment, the very instant that you are in; being aware of how you affect the human social, political, and natural ecology you are a part of and how it affects you. Consciousness is being informed and instructed through your groups peculiar culture on the effects of the varied ecologies on your immediate and distant ancestors, and to be aware of their interpretation of that experience."

—Professor James Small, 1945 - Present

"Other people's opinion of you does not have to become your reality."

"Accept responsibility for your life. Know that it is you who will get you where you want to go, no one else."

—Les Brown, 1945 - Present

"One important key to success is self confidence. An important key to self confidence is preparation. Start where you are. Use what you have. Do what you can."

"My potential is more than can be expressed within the bounds of my race or ethnic identity."

—Arthur Ashe, 1943 - 1993

"Culture is to people as water is to fish, invisible, pervasive and essential."

—Professor Wade Nobles, 1943 - Present

"Many people have serious academic degrees but cannot find a job, and sadly their degrees are so limited that they cannot even think about how to create a job for themselves."

—Haki R. Madhubuti, 1942 - Present

"When the power of love overcomes the love of power, the world will know peace."

—Jimi Hendrix, 1942 - 1970

"A man must be willing to die for justice. Death is an inescapable reality and men die daily, but good deeds live forever."

"Why does the Black man say, 'freedom is doing what I want to do!' and why is it that every thing he 'wants to do' enriches the European?"

"When we get into social amnesia - into forgetting our history - we also forget or misinterpret the history and motives of others as well as our motives. The way to learn of our own creation, how we came to be what we are, is getting to know ourselves. It is through getting to know the self intimately that we get to know the forces that shaped us as a self. Therefore knowing the self becomes a knowledge of the world. A deep study of Black History is the most profound way to learn about the psychology of Europeans and to understand the psychology that flows from their history."

Ultimately, intelligence must be defined in terms of the degree in which it solves YOUR PROBLEMS. The nature of education today prepares you to solve THEIR PROBLEMS and not your own. That's why you study THEIR books, you go to THEIR schools, you learn THEIR information, THEIR language, THEIR styles, THEIR perceptions, so when you come out of school you can do a humdinger of a job solving European problems, but you can't solve your own. And then you DARE call yourself "intelligent?" C'mon. That's the height of stupidity."

The African American community, especially, should vastly overhaul and reconstruct its educational orientation toward knowledge of the Motherland. It must realize that its own economic salvation is coterminous with or tied to that of Africa's. It must invest money and human resources in Africa's development and perceive its economic prosperity as its special responsibility and mission…

—*Dr. Amos Wilson, 1941-1995*

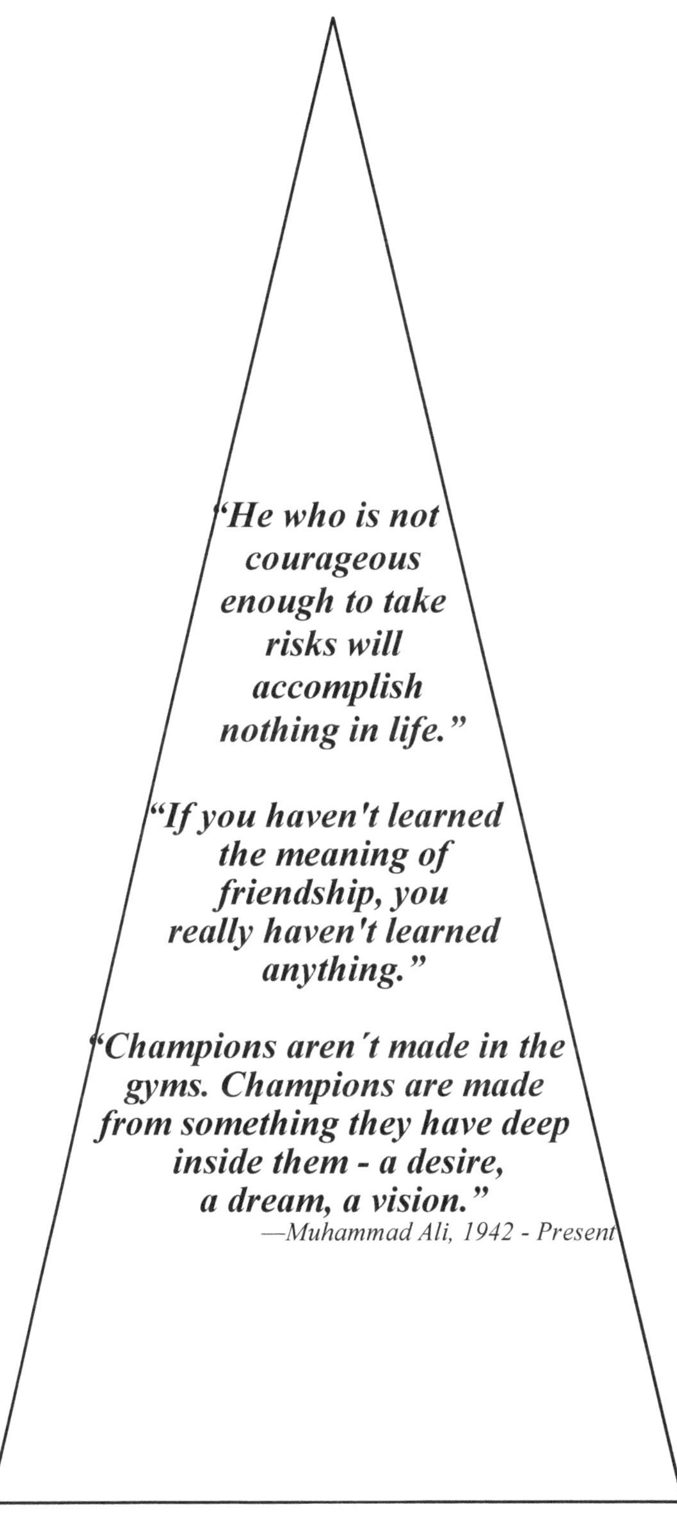
"He who is not
courageous
enough to take
risks will
accomplish
nothing in life."
"If you haven't learned
the meaning of
friendship, you
really haven't learned
anything."
"Champions aren´t made in the
gyms. Champions are made
from something they have deep
inside them - a desire,
a dream, a vision."
—Muhammad Ali, 1942 - Present

"My fear was not of death itself, but a death without meaning."

—Huey P. Newton, 1942 - 1989

"Men who have never received and have had little occasion to express the love theme or original goodness respond in a very significant manner to that real, spontaneous, gratuitous kindness. Those feelings that find no expression in desperate times store themselves up in great abundance, ripen, strengthen and strain the walls of their repository to the utmost; where the kindred spirit touches this wall it crumbles—no one responds to kindness, no one is more sensitive to it than the desperate man."

—George Jackson, Soledad Brothers, 1941 - 1971

"Small wonder our national spirit is husk empty. We have more information but less knowledge. More communication but less community. More goods but less goodwill. More of virtually everything save that which the human spirit requires. So distracted have we become sating this new need or that material appetite, we hardly noticed the departure of happiness."

"The most important office in a democracy is the office of citizen, and it is a responsibility we all have, but we can't practice this office until we become informed."

—Randall Robinson, 1941 - Present

"I am not a perfect servant. I am a public servant doing my best against the odds. As I develop and serve, be patient. God is not finished with me yet."

"If my mind can conceive it, and my heart can believe it, I know I can achieve it."

"In many ways, history is marked as 'before' and 'after' Rosa Parks. She sat down in order that we all might stand up, and the walls of segregation came down."

—Reverend Jessie Louis Jackson, 1941-Present

"The educational system of a country is worthless unless it revolutionizes the social order."

"Philosophers have long conceded, however, that every man has two educators: 'that which is given to him, and the other that which he gives himself. Indeed all that is most worthy in man he must work out and conquer for himself. It is that which constitutes our real and best nourishment. What we are merely taught seldom nourishes the mind like that which we teach ourselves."

"It may be well to repeat here the saying that old men talk of what they have done, young men of what they are doing, and fools of what they expect to do. The Negro race has a rather large share of the last mentioned class."

"The confidence of the people is worth more than money."

—Carter G. Woodson, 1875 - 1950

"Black male and female slaves were brainwashed to see themselves as studs and sexual objects. Many blacks have unconsciously perpetuated the one-dimensional studs and sluts personas."

"Stripped of all self-esteem, slaves clung to the one possession that always mystified, tantalized and angered whites—their sexuality. Black females became sexual objects and black men Mandingo studs. Blackness and hyper-sexuality became inseparable concepts."

"White-on black injustice angers blacks more than black-on-black violence. We should be just as concerned about the injustices we heap on each other as we are with the negative way whites treat us."

"Before and after slavery, blacks were conditioned to believe that whites were mentally, morally and culturally superior. Due to media messaging, African slaves and their descendants have accepted this myth as truth."

"Woven into the black American experience is an abnormal embrace of inaccurate stereotypes created to justify slavery. Damage to our psyches, inherited from societal brainwashing, compels us to accept buffoonery and cling to anything that appeals to our emotions, lightens our mental pain and teaches us to laugh at our own denigration."

"Most blacks are unaware of the psychological trauma resulting from more than 350 years of racial oppression. Even in the so-called 'post-racial era' African Americans still wrestle with the black inferiority complex in the face of white privilege."

—Tom Burrell, 1939– Present

"The first need of a free people is to define their own terms."

"I knew that I could vote and that that wasn't a privilege; it was my right. Every time I tried I was shot, killed or jailed, beaten or economically deprived."

—Kwame Toure (Stokely Carmichael), 1941 - 1998

The last thing Dr. King said to me was, ***"The next movement we will have is to institutionalize and internationalize nonviolence."***

"Sometimes the psychological wounds you get from conditions (segregation, discrimination) takes longer to heal than the physical wounds. Some are permanently scarred by that. We are still getting the residual affects from their older sister and brothers and parents."

"We are moving towards a nonviolent society, and now we must develop the tools to make this possible."

—Dr. Bernard LaFayette, 1940 -Present

"The only thing you're taking out of here is your spirit and your soul, so we need to be conscious to develop that part of ourselves, because we're all spiritual creatures."

—Smokey Robinson, 1940 -Present

"We should not go through this world without making it a better place because we were here."

Martial Art Grandmaster James A. Jones, Jr., 1940—Present

"If you cannot find peace within yourself, you'll never find it anywhere else."

—Marvin Gaye, 1939-1984

"I believe it's our responsibility when we find young, creative people to make their projects our project."

—Lawrence Guyot, 1939-Present

"Science is not something you have to go to a laboratory to do. Life is a lab."

—Walter E. Massey, 1938 -Present

THE LAWS GOVERNING A NONVIOLENT MEETING

1.At the meeting, anyone is allowed to speak. They can only discuss what they and their Creator intend to do. They cannot discuss the misconduct and misfortune of other people, unless they show how that misfortune and/or misconduct creates separation, and unless they explain what they did or are doing to cause reconciliation in the situation, i.e., discuss a healing method for every disorder and misconduct. Otherwise it will be classified as gossip. All flattery is pseudo gossip, an attempt to sophisticate gossip.

2. All references to history should be to prove that there is an intelligent life force that has created all things to live in harmony with each other on earth. (If historical references don't prove the above then the person has a false sense of history which should not be allowed.)

3.Each person must willing to honestly discuss their position, disposition and proposition.

4.The person speaking must be willing and open to let anyone at anytime question their motives and intentions.

5.If one is not prepared to speak under these terms, they must listen, and be contemplative until ready.

6.The songs and music must be the same as the speech.

7.Prayers must be within the framework of the Lord's Prayer and David's 23rd Psalm. The Lord's Prayer is a private request and the 23rd Psalm is the public expression of it. Any prayer vibrations less than this is an outside show to an unfriendly world.

"You cannot use the definition of the slave master to obtain your freedom. Inherent in his definition is your enslavement."

"Racism is the belief that God made a race other than the human race."

"Gangs are guys and gals who don't know government."

—Reverend James Bevel, 1936 - 2008

"You can turn painful situations around through laughter. If you can find humor in anything, even poverty, you can survive it."

"The essence of childhood is play."

—William "Bill" Cosby, 1937-Present

"Success is the result of perfection, hard work, learning from failure, loyalty, and persistence."

—General Colin Powell, 1937-Present

"I don't know the key to success, but the key to failure is trying to please everybody."

"The events which transpired five thousand years ago; Five years ago or five minutes ago, have determined what will happen five minutes from now; five years From now or five thousand years from now. All history is a current event."

"Whoever controls the images, controls your self-esteem, self-respect and self-development. Whoever controls the history, controls the vision."

—Dr. Leonard Jeffries, 1937-Present

I'm a big believer in the fact that life is about preparation, preparation.

–Attorney Johnnie Cochran, 1937 - 2005

"The new science of humaculture is a tool for reversing the effects of slavery by dismantling "the culture that produces poverty, crime, racism, hatred and ineffective education."

—Dr. Nkosi Ajanaku, 1936 – Present

"You don't fight racism with racism, the best way to fight racism is with solidarity."

"You can jail a revolutionary, but you cannot jail the revolution."

"We don't hate nobody because of their color. We hate oppression!"

—Bobby Seale, 1936 - Present

"Respect commands itself and can neither be given nor withheld when it is due."

"The price of hating other human beings is loving oneself less."

—Eldridge Cleaver, 1935 - 1998

"The most important movement now is for education rights."

—Robert "Bob" Moses, 1935 - Present

"You can not make yourself whole again by brooding one hundred percent of the time on the darkness of the world. We are the light of the world."

—Ivan Gladstone Van Sertima, 1935 - 2009

"In a nuclear age we can't afford to be violent, we must be nonviolent."

—Dr. Otis Moss, Sr., 1935 - Present

"We keep going back, stronger, not weaker, because we will not allow rejection to beat us down. It will only strengthen our resolve. To be successful there is no other way."

–Earl Graves

"I never doubted my ability, but when you hear all your life you're inferior, it makes you wonder if the other guys have something you've never seen before. If they do, I'm still looking for it."

"I'm hoping someday that some kid, black or white, will hit more home runs than myself. Whoever it is, I'd be pulling for him."

—Hank Aaron, 1934 - Present

"A man is either free or he is not. There cannot be any apprenticeship for freedom."

"Thought is more important than art. To revere art and have no understanding of the process that forces it into existence, is finally not even to understand what art is."

—Amiri Baraka, 1934 - Present

"You must recognize that the way to get the good out of your brother and your sister is not to return evil for evil."

"If education doesn't bring out what God has put in you for his glory then you're not being properly educated. Education frees you to master yourself."

"Black leadership has to recognize that principles more than speech, character more than a claim, is greater in advancing the cause of our liberation than what has transpired thus far. "

—Minister Louis Farrakhan, 1933 - Present

"We declare our right on this earth...to be a human being, to be respected as a human being, to be given the rights of a human being in this society, on this earth, in this day. Our objective is complete freedom, justice and equality which we intend to bring into existence by any means necessary."

"Education is our passport to the future, for tomorrow belongs to the people who prepare for it today."

"When a person places the proper value on freedom, there is nothing under the sun that he will not do to acquire that freedom. Whenever you hear a man saying he wants freedom, but in the next breath he is going to tell you what he won't do to get it, or what he doesn't believe in doing in order to get it, he doesn't believe in freedom. A man who believes in freedom will do anything under the sun to acquire...or preserve his freedom."

"You can't separate peace from freedom because no one can be at peace unless he has his Freedom."

—El Hajj Malik El Shabazz (Malcolm X), 1925-1965

"Achieving excellence will clearly be a matter of will, not a matter of discovery."

"We must not bring shame on ourselves and upon our descendants. We must bring light to the world again."

—Asa G. Hillard, III—Nana Baffour Amankwatia II, 1933-2007

"Freedom is to move in our intellect to a greater vision, a greater purpose, to a greater responsibility until we are comfortable with ourselves in our life and in our purpose on this earth."

"If we (Black America) become Independent Thinkers, we can make a contribution."

"Man means mind and woman means the womb of mind"

"Freedom is to move" in our intellect to a greater vision, a greater purpose, to a greater responsibility until we are comfortable with ourselves in our life and in our purpose on this earth. ***It's a natural requirement, the life of every human being that their intellect be liberated."***

—Imam W. Deen Mohammed, 1933-2008

"Greatness occurs when your children love you, when your critics respect you and when you have peace of mind."

—Quincy Jones, 1933-Present

"Character is one of most precious parts of you. You can't get involved in things that will damage your character."

–Rod Paige, 7th Secretary of Education, 1933 - Present

"Violence is a tool of the ignorant."

—Flip Wilson, 1933-1998

"My music is the spiritual expression of what I am — my faith, my knowledge, my being … When you begin to see the possibilities of music, you desire to do something really good for people, to help humanity free itself from its hang-ups … I want to speak to their souls."

"All a musician can do is to get closer to the source of nature, and so feel that he is in communion with the natural laws."

"There is never any end. There are always new sounds to imagine. New feelings to get at. And always there is a need to keep purifying these needs and sounds so that we can really see what we've discovered in its pure state, so we can see more clearly what we are. In that way, we can give those who listen to the essence, the best of what we are ."

—John Coltrane, 1926-1967

"In a world where change is inevitable and continuous, the need to achieve that change without violence is essential for survival."

"It is a blessing to die for a cause, because you can so easily die for nothing."

"My hope for my children must be that they respond to the still, small voice of God in their own hearts."

"The purpose of the civil rights struggle was "to seek the human dignity and respect that allows us to live together as brothers and sisters and not perish together as fools."

—Ambassador Andrew Young, 1932-Present

"If it wasn't for Abe Lincoln, I'd still be on the open market."

"Just being a Negro doesn't qualify you to understand the race situation any more than being sick makes you an expert on medicine."

"Civil Rights: What black folks are given in the U.S. on the installment plan, as in civil-rights bills. Not to be confused with human rights, which are the dignity, stature, humanity, respect, and freedom belonging to all people by right of their birth."

—Richard "Dick" Gregory, 1932-Present

"There is not enough magic in a bloodline to forge an instant, irrevocable bond."

—James Earl Jones, 1931-Present

"Now is the time for the U.S. and the nations of Western Europe who engaged in the slave trade throughout this hemisphere to come forward in a positive way to assist in undoing the harm that was caused by their past colonial policies in the hemisphere."

"The challenges African-Americans are facing today are rooted in the system of slavery."

I am struck by how casually we as a nation react to the carnage in Iraq.

–Representative Charles Rangel

"We must join with the tens of millions all over the world who see in peace our most sacred responsibility."

"Through my singing, acting and speaking, I want to make freedom ring. Maybe I can touch people's hearts better than I can their minds, with the common struggle of the common man."

"To be free.. To walk the good American earth as equal citizens, to live without fear, to enjoy the fruits of our toil, to give our children every opportunity in life—that dream which we have held so long in our hearts is today the destiny that we hold in our hands."

"I stand here struggling for the rights of my people to be full citizens in this country and they are not. They are not in Mississippi and they are not . . . in Washington. . . . You want to shut up every Negro who has the courage to stand up and fight for the rights of his people. . . . That is why I am here today. . . ."

—Paul Robeson, 1898 - 1976

"The lack of knowledge of self is a prevailing condition among my people here in America. Gaining the knowledge of self makes us unite into a great unity. Knowledge of self makes you take on the great virtue of learning."

"Mere belief counts for nothing unless carried into practice."

"A nation can rise no higher than its woman."

—The Honorable Elijah Muhammad, 1897 - 1975

"Don't judge yourself by others' standards, have your own. And don't get caught up in the trap of changing yourself to fit the world. The world has to change to fit you. And if you stick to your principles, values and morals long enough, it will."

—Berry Gordy, Jr. 1929-Present

"There will be no revolution until we see Negro faces in all positions that help to mold public opinion, help to shape policy for America."

"Remember that the way to get this revolution off the ground is to forge the moral, spiritual and political pressure which the President, the nation and the world cannot ignore."

–Reverend James Lawson, 1928 – Present

"We must keep in mind that we are not yet 200 years out of slavery and that every effort has been made to destroy Black leadership."

—James R. Forman, 1928—2005

"The Negro will make the gift (a transformed society) when he accepts himself completely—his hair, his skin color, his nose formation, his emotions, his everything."

...a zest for life, a creative capacity for taking hard knocks and transcending them, is a way of life which can save a people who have lost the capacity to enjoy themselves and others because of a Faustian obsession with money and power."

—Lerone, Bennett, 1928—Present

"The role of art isn't just to show life as it is, but to show life as it should be."

—Harry Belafonte, 1927-Present

"Everyday I find something creative to do with my life."

"Don't play what's there, play what's not there."

—Miles Davis, 1926-1991

"We proved we could fly airplanes and do any other job that needed to be done in the military. We showed the whole concept of segregation is a farce. It's not the color of your skin that matters; it's your ability to do the job."

—Dr. John Driver, Tuskegee Airman, 1925 - 2007

"In recognizing the humanity of our fellow beings, we pay ourselves the highest tribute."

"A good teacher must be able to put himself in the place of those who find learning hard."

"Our whole constitutional heritage rebels at the thought of giving government the poser to control men's minds."

"Today's Constitution is a realistic document of freedom only because of several corrective amendments. Those amendments speak to a sense of decency and fairness that I and other Blacks cherish."

—Jurist Thurgood Marshall, 1908 - 1993

I am the darker brother.
They send me to eat in the kitchen
when company comes,
but I laugh, and eat well, and grow strong. Tomorrow,
I'll be at the table when company comes.
Nobody'll dare say to me,
"Eat in the kitchen, then. besides,
They'll see how beautiful I am and be ashamed
I, too, am America.

—Langston Hughes, 1902 - 1967

"Our only hope is to control the vote."
—Medgar Evers, 1925--1963

"I decided in my life that I would do nothing that did not reflect positively on my father's life."
—Sidney Poitier, 1924-Present

"Every struggle makes another struggle necessary."

"It takes radical love to defeat radical evil."
—Reverend C. T. Vivian, 1924 - Present

"Not everything that is faced can be changed, but nothing can be changed until it is faced."
—James A. Baldwin, 1924-1987

"You have to know inside that racism is wrong. You have to know inside that you have the capacity of anyone and given the opportunity, you will overcome."
–Captain Roscoe C. Brow, Jr., Tuskegee Airmen, 1922- Present

"GOD sent me to do this work."
--Reverend Fred Shuttlesworth, 1922 - Present

"There is nothing noble in being superior to somebody else. The only real nobility is in being superior to your former self."

"Support the strong, give courage to the timid, remind the indifferent, and warn the opposed."
—Whitney M. Young, 1921-1971

" We ask you to help us work for that day when black will not be asked to get in back, when brown can stick around, when yellow will be mellow, when the red man can get ahead, man; and when white will embrace what is right."

"If you don't know where you come from, it's difficult to assess where you are. It's even more difficult to plan where you are going."
–Reverend Joseph Lowery, 1921 - Present

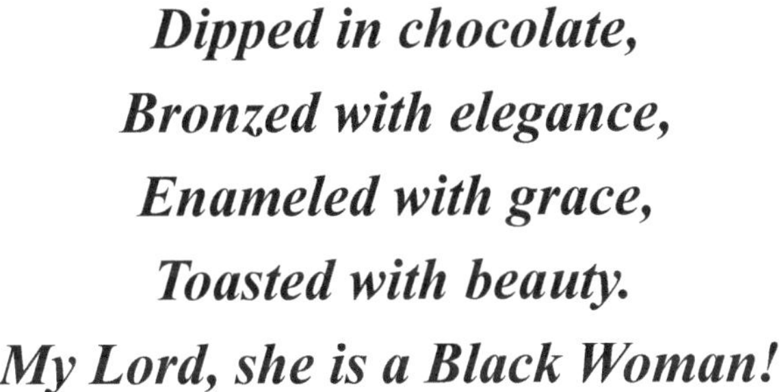

Dipped in chocolate,
Bronzed with elegance,
Enameled with grace,
Toasted with beauty.
My Lord, she is a Black Woman!

—Dr. Yosef Ben Jochannan, 1918 - Present

"God and Nature first made us what we are, and then out of our own created genius we make ourselves what we want to be. Follow always that great law. Let the sky and God be our limit and eternity our measurement."

"When God breathed into the nostrils of man the breath of life, He made him a living soul, and bestowed upon him the authority of "Lord of Creation." He never intended that an individual should descend to the level of a peon, a serf, or a slave, but that he should be always man in the fullest possession of his senses and with the truest knowledge of himself."

"The ends you serve that are selfish will take you no further than yourself but the ends you serve that are for all, in common, will take you into eternity."

"A people without the knowledge of their past history, origin and culture is like a tree without roots."

—Marcus Garvey, 1887 - 1940

"If you pray for one thing, let it be for an idea."

—Percy Sutton, 1920—2009

"I realized by using the high notes of the chords as a melodic line, and by the right harmonic progression, I could play what I heard inside me. That's when I was born."

"Music is your own experience, your own thoughts, your wisdom. If you don't live it, it won't come out of your horn. They teach you there's a boundary line to music. But, man, there's no boundary line."

—Charlie Parker, 1920 - 1955

"To succeed, one must be creative and persistent."

"Failure is a word I don't accept."

"Dream small dreams. If you make them too big, you get overwhelmed and you don't do anything. If you make small goals and accomplish them, it gives you the confidence to go on to higher goals."

"You spend so much time in your profession it ought to be something you love."

—John H. Johnson, 1919 - 1972

"It's not happenstance at birth or color of skin. It's about content of character."

–Lt. Col. Lee Archer, Tuskegee Airmen, 1919 - 2010

"I may be helping to bring harmony between people through my music."

"Get me well so I can get on television and tell people to stop smoking."

—Nat King Cole, 1919 - 1965

"It is important for young people to be exposed to as many areas of learning as possible so that they can decide what they want to do."

—Dr. David Blackwell, 1919 - 2010

Rules For Living

1. Save a part of all you earn and pay yourself first.
2. Establish a reputation at a bank. Save at an established institution and borrow there. Stay away from loan sharks.
3. Take no chances with your money. A man who can't afford to lose has no business gambling.
4. Never borrow anything that, if forced to it, you can't pay back.
5. Don't get bigheaded with the little fellows.
6. Don't have so much pride.
7. Find a need and fill it. Successful businesses are founded on the needs of the people.
8. Stay in your own class. Never run around with people you can't compete with.
9. Once you get money people will give you money.
10. Once you reach a certain bracket, it is very difficult not to make more money.

"Money is no good unless it contributes something to the community, unless it builds a bridge to a better life. Any man can make money, but it takes a special kind of man to use it responsibly."

"When you get you a good wife, you love her."

—A.G. Gaston, 1892-1996

"Fear of something is at the root of hate for others, and hate within will eventually destroy the hater."

"Since new developments are the products of a creative mind, we must therefore stimulate and encourage that type of mind in ever way possible."

"When you can do the common things of life in an uncommon way, you will command the attention of the world."

"When I was young, I said to God, "God, tell me the mystery of the universe." But God answered, that knowledge is for me alone. So I said, "God, tell me the mystery of the peanut." Then God said, well, George, that's more nearly your size."

—Dr. George Washington Carver, 1864 - 1943

"Life is not a spectator sport. If you're going to spend your whole life in the grandstand just watching what goes on, in my opinion you're wasting your life."

"You can kill a man but you can't kill an idea."

"A life is not important except in the impact it has on other lives."

—Jackie Robinson, 1919 - 1972

"I find in being black, a thing of beauty; a joy; a strength; a secret cup of gladness."

"Any form of art is a form of power; it has impact, it can affect change - it can not only move us, it makes us move."

—Ossie Davis, 1917 - 2005

"...education has but one honorable purpose, everything else is a waste of time, that is to train the student to be a proper handler of power."

"You have to make a distinction between an organized religion and a spiritual way of life."

"You start building a nation by creating the things that are essential to your existence."

—Dr. John Henrik Clarke, 1915 - 1998

"When I discover who I am, I'll be free."

"Power doesn't have to show off. Power is confident, self-assuring, self-starting, self-stopping, self-warming and self-justifying. When you have it, you know it."

—Ralph Ellison, 1914 -1994

Ebon Venus

Let others boast of maidens fair of eyes of blue and golden hair!
My heart like need is ever true turns to the maid of ebon hue.
I love her form of matchless grace. the dark brown beauty of her face.
Her lips that speak of love'd delight Her eyes that gleam as stars at night.
O'er Venus let them rage, Who sets the fashion of the age;
Each to his taste, but as for me,
My Venus shall be ebony.

—Lewis Latimer, 1848-1928

"The battles that count are not the ones for the gold metals. The struggles within yourself - the invisible, inevitable battles within all of us, that's where its at."

"Find the good. It's all around you. Find it, showcase it and you'll start believing in it."

"We all have dreams, but in order to make dreams come into reality, it takes an awful lot of determination, dedication, self-discipline, and effort."

—Jessie Owens, 1913 - 1980

"My own opinion was that blacks could best overcome racist attitudes through achievements, even though those achievements had to take place within the hateful environment of segregation."

—General Benjamin Oliver Davis Jr., 1912 - 2002

"When I say I love Eastland, it sounds preposterous--a man who brutalizes people. But "you" love him or you wouldn't be here. You're going to Mississippi to create social change--and you love Eastland in your desire to create conditions which will redeem his children. Loving your enemy is manifest in putting your arms not around the man but around the social situation, to take power from those who misuse it--at which point they can become human too"

—Bayard Rustin, 1912 - 1987

"The guy who takes a chance, who walks the line between the known and unknown, who is unafraid of failure, will succeed."

—Gordon Parks, 1912 - Present

"Freedom is an internal achievement rather than an external adjustment."

"A man's respect for law and order exists in precise relationship to the size of his paycheck."

"In my preaching the shafts are ever aimed at the brainwashed horde."

—Congressman Adam Clayton Powell, 1908 - 1972

"It is rather hard to be accused of shiftlessness and idleness when the accuser closes the avenue of labor and industrial pursuits to us."

"It is an undisputed fact that the Negro vote in the State of Alabama, as well as most of the other Southern States, have been effectively suppressed, either one way or the other--in some instances by constitutional amendment and State legislation, in others by cold-blooded fraud and intimidation, but whatever the method pursued, it is not denied, but frankly admitted in the speeches in this House, that the black vote has been eliminated to a large extent."

—George Henry White, 1852– 1918

"If you want the civilization of a people to reach the very best elements of their being, and then, having reached them, there to abide, as an indigenous principle, you must imbue the womanhood of that people with all its elements and qualities. Any movement which passes by the female sex is an ephemeral thing. Without them, no true nationality, patriotism, religion, cultivation, family life, or true social status is a possibility. In this matter it takes two to make one- mankind is a duality. The male may bring, as an exotic, a foreign graft, say of a civilization, to a new people. But what then? Can a graft live or thrive of itself? By no manner of means. It must get vitality from the stock into which it is put; and it is the women who gives the sap to every human organization which thrives and flourishes on earth."

"Let our posterity know that we their ancestors, uncultured and unlearned, amid all trials and temptations, were men of integrity."

"Those too impressed with material things cannot hold their place n the world of culture; they are relegated to inferiority and ultimate death."

"Strive to make something of yourself; then strive to make the most of yourself."

—Rev. Alexander Crummell, 1819 - 1898

"Violence is a personal necessity for the oppressed. It is not a strategy consciously devised. It is the deep, instinctive expression of a human being denied individuality."

—Richard N. Wright, 1908 - 1960

"No matter how hopeless the situation is, you've got to continue to struggle. You might lose, but if you don't struggle you certainly won't win."

—John G. Jackson, 1907 - 1993

"Excellence of performance will transcend artificial barriers created by man."

—Dr. Charles Drew, 1904 - 1950

"We must fight as a race for everything that makes for a better country and a better world. We are dreaming idiots and trusting fools to do anything less."

—Ralph Bunche, 1904 -1971

"Negro school" is obsolete. The need today, is far greater. It is worldwide understanding based on the concept of brotherhood. Nowhere is there a university designed and equipped [so well] to make this ambitious aim a reality."

—Horace Mann Bond, 1904 – 1972

"The talk of winning our share is not the easy one of disengagement and flight, but the hard one of work, of short as well as long jumps, of disappointments, and of sweet success."

—Roy Wilkins, 1901 - 1981

"What we play is life."

"We all do 'do, re, mi,' but you have got to find the other notes yourself."

"There is no such thing as 'on the way out' as long as you are still doing something interesting and good; you're in the business because you're breathing"

—Lousi Armstrong, 1901 - 1971

"Presumption should never make us neglect that which appears easy to us, nor despair make us lose courage at the sight of difficulties."

"I am of the African race, and in the color which is natural to them of the deepest dye; and it is under a sense of the most profound gratitude to the Supreme Ruler of the Universe."

—Benjamin Banneker, 1731- 1806

"What seems to have escaped the generality of writers and commentators is that all three forms of government are identical in having regimented life from top to bottom, in having ruthlessly suppressed freedom of speech, assembly, press and thought, and in being controlled by politicians...The politician being the only class in society that is charlatan enough to offer a cure for everything if elected to office."

"On the horizon loom a growing number of iconoclasts and Atheists, young black men and women who can read, think, and ask questions, and who impertinently demand to know why Negroes should revere a God who permits them to be lynched, Jim-crowed and disfranchised."

—George S. Schuyler, 1895—1977

"Idealism is like a castle in the air if it is not based on a solid foundation of social and political realism."

"If a man is not faithful to his own individuality, he cannot be loyal to anything."

"I feel that my own good country robbed me of the chance for some of the great experiences that I would have liked to live through."

"I would forever fight to keep hope alive."

—Percy Levon Julian, 1899 -1975

"I encourage young Black undergraduates to pursue mathematic studies at the graduate level."

—Dr. Elbert F. Cox, 1895—1969

"At best, race is a superstition."

"Every man and woman is born into the world to do something unique and something distinctive and if he or she does not do it, it will never be done."

"The tragedy of life doesn't lie in not reaching your goal. The tragedy lies in having no goal to reach. It isn't a calamity to die with dreams unfilled, but it is a calamity not to dream. It is not disgrace to reach the stars, but it is a disgrace to have no stars to reach for. Not failure, but low aim, is a sin."

"He who starts behind in the great rice of life must forever remain behind or run faster that the man in front."

—Benjamin E. Mays, 1894-1984

"The Negro people of America... have cut our forests, tilled our fields, built our railroads, fought our battles, and in all of their trials they have manifested a simple faith, a grateful heart, a cheerful spirit, and an undivided loyalty. Now they have come to the place where their faith can no longer feed on the bread of repression and violence. They ask for the bread of liberty, of public equality, and public responsibility. It must not be denied them."

"I know the dark delight of being strange. The penalty of difference in the crowd. The loneliness of wisdom among fools . . ."

—Claude McKay, 1890-1948

"Western civilization, Christianity, decency are struggling for their very lives. In this worldwide civil war, race prejudice is our most dangerous enemy, for it is a disease at the very root of our democratic life."

—Dr. Mordecai Johnson, 1890– 1976

"A community is democratic only when the humblest and weakest person can enjoy the highest civil, economic, and social rights that the biggest and most powerful possess."

"Justice is never given; it is exacted and the struggle must be continuous for freedom is never a final fact, but a continuing evolving process to higher and higher levels of human, social, economic, political and religious relationship."

—A. Philip Randolph, 1889 - 1979

"Money does not make the man and clothes do not make the man. It is character and free national standards that make the man."

—Noble Drew Ali, Moorish Science Temple of America, 1886 - 1929

"For generations the Negro has been the peasant matrix of that section of America which has most undervalued him, and here he has contributed not only materially in labor and in social patience, but spiritually as well. The South has unconsciously absorbed the gift of his folk-temperament. In less than half a generation it will be easier to recognize this, but the fact remains that a leaven of humor, sentiment, imagination and tropic nonchalance has gone into the making of the South from a humble, unacknowledged source."

—Alain Locke, 1886 - 1954

"Negro authors, once they free their art of the necessity of furnishing the means of life, will drop the stereotypes into limbo with the assurance that real art will finally create in their readers a demand for honest treatment of every gradation of Negro life."

"Show me a population that is deeply religious, and I will show you a servile population, content with whips and chains, contumely and the gibbet, content to eat the bread of sorrow and drink the waters of affliction."

—Hubert H. Harrison, 1883 - 1927

"Ethiopians, that is, Negroes, gave the world the first idea of right and wrong and thus laid the basis of religion and all true culture and civilization."

"The doctrine of inequality is emphatically a science of white people. It is they who invented it."

—J. A. Rogers, 1880 - 1966

"Love is the answer
At least for most of the questions in my heart
Why are we here and where do we go
And how come it's so hard
It's not always easy and sometimes life can be deceiving
I'll tell you one thing
It's always better when we're together."

—Jack Johnson, 1878 - 1946

"If you can be the best, then why not try to be the best."

—Garrett Morgan, 1877 - 1963

"I know why the caged bird sings, ah me, when his wing is bruised and his bosom sore; when he beats his bars and he would be free, it is not a carol of joy or glee, but a prayer that he sends from his heart's deep core."

"The Lord had a job for me, but I had so much to do, I said, "You get somebody else--or wait till I get through." I don't know how the Lord came out, but He seemed to get along: But I felt kinda sneakin' like, 'cause I know'd I done Him wrong. One day I needed the Lord--Needed Him myself--needed Him right away, And He never answered me at all, but I could hear Him say Down in my accusin' heart, "Nigger, I'se got too much to do, You get somebody else or wait till I get through."

—Paul Lawrence Dunbar, 1872 - 1906

"My friends made fun of me...they thought it was foolish of me to anticipate success in a field in which so many men before me had failed, but I went on fighting the opposition of my adversaries and the indifference of my friends, and emerged victorious but battle-scarred."

"No greater glory, no greater honor, is the lot of man departing than a feeling possessed deep in his heart that the world is a better place for his having lived."

—Robert Sengstacke Abbott, 1870 - 1940

SOME OF THE ELEMENTS OF A GENUINE AND PERMANENT PROGRESS.

FIRST. There must be the desire for better. This desire implies a recognition of imperfection-- a knowledge of deficiency...
SECOND. The desire will avail nothing, if there be no movement. When the prodigal son came to himself, realized that is, his condition, and the intense desire for a better state of things was awakened in his soul, he said, " I will arise and go to my father," and he arose and went. There is little use in the most ardent prayers, and even in the exceeding bitter cry, if there is no movement.
THIRD and an essential element of permanent progress is righteousness.
The successful man of business is he who is endowed with ... a sense of order, of the value of time, a presence of mind in difficulty, a power of seeing the thing to be done at the proper time, insight into the relations of different kinds of wealth. These are the qualities which have filled this land and Europe with the magnates of riches. This is a bettering of the outward conditions.

"The elements of usefulness and permanence are lacking where the man of money has no proper idea of his possessions, when he uses them only for himself - only to get on - only to push forward his family or his friends: with no larger aim for the interests of the community and when he has advanced in years he will have wearied old age, magnificence and splendor in his outward surroundings, but no largeness of heart-- forgotten, and justly forgotten, the day after his death."

"Everybody knows that the basis of the civilization and literature of present day was on the Nile and not among the Caucasian race - not on the Ilissus, the Tiber, the Rhine or the Thames, but on the rivers of Ethiopia. There were only two steps between Egypt and modern Europe - Greece and Rome. Greece took not only civilization and literature but even religion from Ethiopia. Such were the wonderful developments of civilization and literature and religion in that country, that the early poets and historians of Greece, unable to understand such marvelous indigenous growth attributed it to the direct interference of the gods, who they affirm went every year to feast with the Ethiopians."

—Edward Wilmot Blyden, 1832-1912

"Now is the accepted time, not tomorrow, not some more convenient season. It is today that our best work can be done and not some future day or future year. It is today that we fit ourselves for the greater usefulness of tomorrow. Today is the seed time, now are the hours of work, and tomorrow comes the harvest and the playtime."

"The power of the ballot we need in sheer defense, else what shall save us from a second slavery?"

"Playing the man" included a resolve "to stand straight, look the world squarely in the eye, and walk to my work with no shuffle or slouch... to refuse to cringe in body or in soul, to resent deliberate insult, and assert my just rights in the face of wanton aggression."

—W. E. DuBois, 1868 - 1963

"As I stood there on the top of the world and I thought of the hundreds of men who had lost their lives in the effort to reach it [North Pole], I felt profoundly grateful that I had the honor of representing my race."

"I think I'm the first man to sit on top of the world."

—Matthew Henson, 1866 – 1955

"The highest test of the civilization of any race is in its willingness to extend a helping hand to the less fortunate."

"Success is to be measured not so much by the position that one has reached in life as by the obstacles which he has overcome."

"Associate yourself with people of good quality, for it is better to be alone than in bad company."

"One man cannot hold another man down in the ditch without remaining down in the ditch with him."

—Booker T. Washington, 1856-1915

"I believe I can do anything if I try."

—Granville T. Woods, 1856 - 1910

"Anything is possible, when it is done in love, and everything you can do should be in love or it will fail."

—Daniel Hale Williams, 1856-1931

"I do not care how dark the night; I believe in the coming of the morning."

—Dr. Joseph Charles Price 1854-1893)

He said little if anything to us. Off the record, he said everything that ever was of value or worth.

"Courage, dignity, endurance, integrity, intelligence."

It is difficult to imagine a priority of human values which he did not demonstrate, and all under the circumstances configured to suppress and devalue.

—Edward Bouchet, First African American Doctorate, 1852-1918

"It is easier to build strong children than to repair broken men."

"I prefer to be true to myself, even at the hazard of incurring the ridicule of others, rather than to be false, and to incur my own abhorrence."

"The soul that is within me no man can degrade."

"I would unite with anybody to do right and with nobody to do wrong."

"America is false to the past, false to the present, and solemnly binds herself to be false to the future."

"No man can put a chain about the ankle of his fellow man without at last finding the other end fastened about his own neck."

"Without a struggle there can be no progress."

–Frederick Douglas, 1818 - 1885

"In every man's mind, the good seeds of liberty are planted, and he who brings his fellow down so low, as to make him contented with a condition of slavery, commits the highest crime against God and man."

"The orators and statesmen of our land, whether they belong to the past, or to the present, will live and shine in the annals of history, in proportion as they have dedicated their genius and talents to the defense of Justice and man's God-given rights."

"Rather die freemen than live to be slaves."

"The humblest peasant is as free in the sight of God as the proudest monarch that ever swayed a scepter. Liberty is a spirit sent from God and like its great Author is no respecter of persons."

–Henry Highland Grant, 1815 - 1882

"We must make an issue, create an event, and establish a national position for ourselves, and never may expect to be respected as men and women, until we have undertaken some fearless, bold and adventurous deeds of daring…"

"Every people should be originators of their own destiny."

"Our elevation must be the result of self-efforts and work of our own hands. No other human power can accomplish it. If we but decide it shall be, it will be so."

–Dr. Martin Delaney, 1812 - 1885

"Having soon discovered to be great, I must appear so, and therefore studiously avoided mixing in society, and wrapped myself in mystery, devoting my time to fasting and prayer."

"What right did white men have to treat me like an ox simply because I am black when an indomitable soul within is as good as they."

–Reverend Nat Turner, 1800 - 1831

"My brother and sisters were bid off first...my mother, paralyzed with grief, held me by the hand. Her turn came and she was bought. Then I was offered...My mother, half distracted with the thought of parting forever from all her children, pushed through the crowd while the bidding for me was going on, to the spot where Riley was standing. She fell at his feet, and clung to his knees, entreating him in tones that a mother could only command, to buy her baby as well as herself, and spare to her one, of her little ones. This man disengaged himself from her with violent blows and kicks."

"We lodged in huts and on the bare ground. Wooden floors were an unknown luxury. In a single room were huddled, like cattle, ten or a dozen persons, men, women, and children. All ides of refinement and decency were of course out of the question."

–Josiah Henson, 1789 - 1883

"I thank my God, that through a long life of hardship and adversity, I have ever been free in both mind and body: and have always raised my voice on behalf of my enslaved countrymen."

—Reverend Robert Wedderburn, 1762 - 1835

"If you love your children, if you love your country, if you love the God of love, clear your hands from slaves, burden not your children or country with them."

"We deemed it expedient to have a form of discipline, whereby we may guide our people in the fear of God, in the unity of the Spirit, and in the bonds of peace, and preserve us from that spiritual despotism which we have so recently experienced--remembering that we are not to lord it over God's heritage, as greedy dogs that can never have enough. But with long suffering, and bowels of compassion to bear each other's burdens, and so fulfill the Law of Christ, praying that our mutual striving together for the promulgation of the Gospel may be crowned with abundant success."

–Richard Allen, 1760 - 1831

"I was born a slave, but nature gave me the soul of a free man…."

—Toussaint L'Ouverture, 1743 - 1803

Those of you who can read I must beg you to read the Bible, and whenever you can get time, study the Bible, and if you can get no other time, spare some of your time from sleep, and learn what the mind and will of God is.

—Jupiter Hammon, 1711 – 1806

STUDY GUIDE

1..Choose four favorite quotes. Make a poster of them and put it up where you can see them daily.

2. Do research on those people you don't know. Find out what inspired them to say what they did.

3. Share these quotes with family and friends.

4. Interpret these quotes in your own words. Break them down and make sense out of them for you.

5. Use these quotes when you speak, whether in public or too your friends.

6. Send text messages and put the quotes on your facebook page.

7. Do a volunteer school report on one or more of these personages.

8. Apply these sayings to your life, make them meaningful.

9. Write and essay on what these quotes mean to you and email it to us. We want to hear from you and may post it on our website.

10. Give this book as a gift to those who need to be uplifted.

Order In Bulk

Inspirational & Wisdom Sayings of African American Men

And

Inspirational & Wisdom Sayings of African American Women

Bulk orders accepted. For quote information email rush2freedom@gmail.com or call (202) 527-9798

The Nonviolent Right To Vote Movement People's Almanac

47th Anniversary Edition

Compiled By

Helen L. Bevel

Published by

The Institute for the Study & Advancement of Nonviolence

This book/almanac presents the people, places, actions and facts, about how nonviolence was applied to the civil rights movement to bring about the Voting Rights Act of 1965. It is a compelling journey through time, presenting the history of a people and the events that led to the historic Selma Right To Vote Movement of 1965. It also presents a dynamic case for why and how nonviolence can be used to address personal and inter-personal problems, issues and concerns (bullying, war between the sexes, suicide, identity crisis, neighborhood empowerment, conflict resolution and much more).

This is a history book for children and adults. It provides a clear understanding of how nonviolence as a strategy was used to overcome social problems and it challenges us to use it to solve personal and inter-personal problems, the new frontier. It gives young people of all ages and races a rich history that provides hope that they can built on to create meaningful and productive lives.

Each year leading up to the Golden Jubilee in 2015 more and more content will be added to each edition as unsung "Heroes and Sheroes" are included to create a complete picture of those who made this movement a success and part of their history and struggles.

Every family, school, church, business and organization that has a commitment to the advancement and achievement of African American people, thus America, should have a copy of this book so that they can know and share the facts about what happened. In this way young people in your charge can build on this monumental achievement in overcoming the great obstacles to freedom. The success of nonviolence in this overcoming means that there is nothing that cannot be overcome when it is understood and used strategically.

"It's either nonviolence or nonexistence."

"We have overcome. Now let us continue to move forward by choosing the weapon of victory assured, nonviolence. To abandon nonviolence is to throw away the gains that our ancestors sacrificed, suffered, bled and died to achieve. In that nonviolence gained us the victory, it stands to reason that in order to maintain these rich achievements, we must employ nonviolence in all areas of our living; personal, inter-personal, social and environmental. In this we create a new foundation for institutional development and civilized living. This is a paradigm shift from the old, antiquated, co-dependent, outdated, violent based model. Which side are you on?"

The Sponsorship Edition Of

The Nonviolent Right To Vote Movement People's Almanac

provides a way for any person or institution to become a part of this rich history, and a means by which we can distribute freely to schools and libraries. Sponsor a listing for $250 or pages (of various sizes). Place a bid for sponsorship of the back cover and/or inside front or back cover. For more information please visit our website.

515 Pages	Pictures
Includes:	Posters
Articles	Quotes
Charts	Quiz's
Historical Documents	Timelines
Personal Histories	Therapies

The Sponsorship
Right To Vote Movement People's Almanac

Be A Part of the Rich History of The Nonviolent Movement

Sponsor A Listing

Listing & Logo Sponsorship of the 47th Anniversary Edition
Listing, Logo, Back Cover, Inside Front & Back Sponsorship
48th, 49th & 50th Edition

Sponsorship Editions will be priced at $10 each and individuals, libraries and schools can register for a free copy.

Preview at: **http://issuu.com/freedomgirl/docs/almanac**

Purchase at: **http://lulu.com/myeka**

Publisher Website: **http://almanac.2freedom.com**

For information or bulk orders email or call:
nonviolentstudy@gmail.com ▪ (773) 413 - 0081

Please visit our website for exciting offers.

www.ingramcontent.com/pod-product-compliance
Ingram Content Group UK Ltd.
Pitfield, Milton Keynes, MK11 3LW, UK
UKHW041839200726
13854UKWH00003BA/1217